aMUSE

Chair, National Board of Directors
Kathy Hopinkah Hannan

Interim Chief Executive Officer
Judith Batty

Vice President, Program Strategy and Development
Savita Raj

girl scouts

the dove self-esteem fund

Photographs

Page 14: Joanne DeNaut with Pultzer Prize winning playwright Nilo Cruz; **Page 26:** Victor Baldizon/Getty Images; **Pages 34 & 35:** Gabriella Miotto; **Page 40:** Anne-Christine Poujoulat Stringer/Getty Images; **Page 41:** Phil Weymouth/Getty Images; **Page 41:** AFP/Getty Images; **Page 41:** New York Daily News Archive/Getty Images; **Page 62:** courtesy of Alchemy Caterers; **Page 64:** courtesy of the PE.com; **Page 65:** courtesy of SCR/James and the Giant Peach sketches by Angela Calin; **Pages 70 & 71:** images and photos from READ MY PINS, Stories from a Diplomat's Jewel Box by Madeleine K. Albright (Harper) Photographs by John Bigelow Taylor; **Page 75:** Andy Sotiriou/Getty Images; **Page 75:** Erik Isakson/Getty Images; **Page 75:** K-King Photography Media Co. Ltd/Getty Images; **Page 75:** Alvis Upitis/Getty Images

This publication was made possible by a generous grant from the Dove Self-Esteem Fund.

SENIOR DIRECTOR, PROGRAM RESOURCES: Suzanne Harper

ART DIRECTOR: Douglas Bantz

WRITER: Valerie Takahama

CONTRIBUTOR: Andrea Bastiani Archibald

EXECUTIVE EDITOR: Laura J. Tuchman

ILLUSTRATORS: Megan Eplett, Faith Erin Hicks (comic artist), Helen Dardik, Jing Jing Tsong

DESIGNER: Charlyne Fabi, Right Hat LLC for Charette Communications, Inc.

ART AND DESIGN: Ellen Kelliher, Sheryl O'Connell, Sarah Micklem, Lesley Williams

FSC
www.fsc.org
MIX
Paper from responsible sources
FSC® C011825

The women mentioned in this book are examples of how women have used their voice in the world. This doesn't mean that GSUSA (or you) will agree with everything they have ever done or said.

Table of Contents

Think of All the Roles You Play Every Day

You're a girl, a student, and a Girl Scout Junior.
You may also be a singer, writer, athlete, chef,
money manager, tech whiz, painter, fashion stylist—
maybe even a diva, if you'd ever admit it!

But there's still so much more to your story!
What other roles do you want to try?

ey manager girl
; chef tech whiz
list athlete yogi
t junior dancer
ainter collector

How about an **Olympic athlete**, or
a **jet pilot**, or a **professional dancer**,
or a **crime-solving detective**?

What would it be like to run a fashion magazine, and
be the one who decides what clothes to photograph?
Or be a **veterinarian**, or the **town mayor**, or an
engineer who finds a solution to pollution?

Would these roles change the story you could tell
about yourself? Would they change how you feel about
yourself? Would you feel stronger? Would you walk
taller? Would you speak more confidently? There's only
one way to find out!

**This journey called a*MUSE*
is all about stories.** It's also
all about having fun trying
on roles, and being a leader
who stretches herself to play
new parts. You'll be turning
acting into action, too, by
inspiring others toward their
best roles ever! Inspiring
others for the better—that's
the story of Girl Scouts!

So places, everyone!
The orchestra's tuning up.
The curtain's about to rise.
Get ready to take the
spotlight in one of the
greatest stories of all—
the story of you!

Your Aha! Moments Are Coming!

Chances are you've been to a **muse**um. You've told funny stories to **amuse** your friends. You've sung songs, danced, and listened to **mus(e)**-ic! How are all these connected? By muses! And who or what are muses?

Originally, muses weren't real people. They were like guides with special powers. They helped creative people put their imaginations to work—they got them inspired and fired up! Muses put the *"ah"* in those *aha!* moments.

In ancient times, people believed there were three Muses, or goddesses, each with her own creative area to oversee. Thalia kept watch over comedy. Terpsichore looked after dance. Calliope inspired very long story poems.

When an artist cried, "O, Muse!" she was really saying, "I need help!" And faster than you could say "aha!" that help arrived like a giant burst of inspiration. Aha! moments will be coming for you, too, all along this a*MUSE* journey.

The Muses and You

Today, a muse can be anyone or anything that inspires you.

Along this journey you'll meet many inspiring women and girls. One of them is Mitali Perkins. She writes children's books and spends a lot of time in schools and libraries talking about growing up in two different cultures and the life-changing power of storytelling. Mitali's own story and the strong female characters in her books inspire girls everywhere! (For more on Mitali, see page 51.)

You're probably good at telling stories, too. After all, your life is filled with excitement, drama, laughs, adventures, setbacks, and triumphs, just like any good story in a movie, play, TV show, or book. Do you have an imaginative guide who inspires you? And, as you take this journey, think about who you inspire!

Muse Who?

The names of those ancient muses are a mouthful, aren't they?

Thalia is pronounced tha LIE ya

Terpsichore rhymes with hickory: terp SIK or ee

Calliope is said as ca LIE o pee

And by the way, to muse means "to think." You'll be *muse*-ing all through a*MUSE*.

We're your aMUSE-ing Muses. I'm Thalia. Just call me ALIA.

I'm COREY—that's short for Terpsichore. I bet you already have a muse, but don't know it.

And I'm Calliope, but everyone calls me CALLIE.

ARE YOU MY MUSES? Can't I have eight? One for each arm and leg!

Awards Along the Journey

On a*MUSE*, you can earn three important awards. These awards move you up the Girl Scout leadership ladder and give you the skills you need to go for the Girl Scout Bronze Award!

Here they are:

Reach Out!

Reach out to women and girls to explore the many roles they play in the world around you, and the leadership skills they use to play them.

Speak Out!

Speak out against stereotypes by:

✦ identifying a stereotype that could hold you or others back from trying on roles in life

✦ teaming up to create a story about this stereotype, and

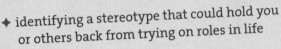

✦ sharing your story to inspire other people (kids, adults, whoever you choose!) to help you stop the stereotyping.

To earn the awards, follow the steps in your **aMUSE Award Tracker** on pages 76–78. And look for pictures of all the awards in your book. They point to fun activities that will get you going toward the awards.

Try Out!

Try out many roles, and make a promise to keep trying out new roles as a leader in life.

8

If you earn all three awards, and you put them together, you'll get an aMUSE-ing finale like this.

REACH OUT

SPEAK OUT

TRY OUT

Ta-da!

ACT 1, Scene 1
All About Roles

Look around you at all the roles played by people you see or talk to every day. Look at all the fictional characters around you, too. Imagine what it would be like to switch places with any of these people and do what they do. Actors and storytellers take on roles—and you can, too!

Your Favorite Roles

Singers, spies, princesses, friendly witches, adventurers . . .

All kinds of exciting roles fill TV shows, movies, books, video games, and the Internet. They're in TV commercials and ads, too—on billboards, on the sides of buses, in magazines, and on the Web. Roles for girls are everywhere!

Maybe you know about a girl named Ella who had a spell cast upon her and had to do everything she was told. Or maybe you've read about the very logical, very brilliant Hermione Granger, who's friends with Harry Potter. Or how about that girl named Fern who rescues a pig named Wilbur, who makes friends with an intelligent spider named Charlotte, who . . . well, you probably know the rest. These are fictional characters—you know that, too. They all have a role to play.

Who are your FIVE favorite ~~girl~~ characters, and what roles do they play?

1

Character: ~~xxxxxxxx~~ Bell

Role: ~~xxxxx~~ Princess

2

Character: Annemarie | baby yoda

Role: freind | HERO

3

Character: Boss baby

Role: Manager (CEO?)

4

Character: Fluffy eliphant

Role: Serial Killer

5

Character: chicken cats ~~xxxx~~ (moana)

Role:

Now use your favorite girl characters to think up a NEW character.

She can play whatever role you want. Maybe she'll blend all the qualities you admire in your favorite characters. Or maybe she'll be someone totally different—the kind of girl character you've never seen but have always wanted to know.

Draw or write what you like about your new character, and then answer these questions:

What can she do that you can do, too?

....

....

....

What's one quality she has that you don't have, but wish you did? Why?

....

....

....

....

Now give this new character of yours a theme song!

Pretend you're in charge of choosing the music for a movie, TV show, or play. That's the role of a composer. So be a composer for your character. What music matches her personality? (Is she energetic and bouncy? Mysterious and dramatic? Dreamy and gentle?) Think of a song that puts you in the mood of your character. Or make up your own!

Write your song's title here:

....

And while you're at it, why not give yourself a theme song, too?

....

13

A Cheerleader for Actors

Have you ever read a book and then pictured in your mind the actress who'd be perfect to play the heroine in the movie version?

That's similar to what a casting director does. She starts with the script or screenplay, the written version of the story that's going to be performed—whether it's a movie, TV show, video, play, or commercial. Then she gets together with the director, and sometimes the writer, to decide what kinds of actors might be best for the roles. She then puts out a "casting call" to give actors a chance to read from the script to try out for the part. The actors might only get 10 minutes to make a good impression!

Casting director Joanne DeNaut, in her office in California

"It comes down to who really captures the character in this little bit of time," says **Joanne DeNaut**, the casting director for South Coast Repertory, a professional theater company in Costa Mesa, California.

DeNaut sees herself as a cheerleader for the actors. "You want them to succeed, and they need to know that," she says. That's a good thing to remember when you're in charge of putting together a cast, or any kind of group, including a sports team. In fact, wanting others to succeed is an important trait of all successful leaders!

Acting Tip: Breathe...

Actors sometimes get the jitters before an audition. Do you get them, too, when you're performing a role? Deep breathing can calm you down.

Try this!

Stand or sit up straight and relax your shoulders.

Then breathe in a full, deep breath through your nose. Feel the air fill your chest.

Hold that breath for a moment. Then exhale slowly and fully through your mouth.

Try it two more times.

Listening to what your body tells you when you're tired or hungry can help you perform better, too. Getting a good night's sleep and eating healthful snacks, like fresh fruits and vegetables, can make for an award-winning performance in any role!

Keep a Casting

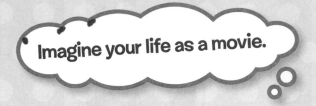

Imagine your life as a movie.

Keep your own Casting Call Log to track the many women you encounter each day. Try it for a few days, or a week or two.

Think about the roles all the women in your life play. Some take care of your basic needs by providing you with food, shelter, clothing, ways to stay healthy, and ways to get where you need to be. Some give you encouragement, teach you new things, or challenge you to stretch your abilities. Some keep your community running smoothly—they direct traffic, repair streets and buildings, deliver the mail, and decide cases in court.

Name	Role(s) ~~she~~ *they* plays	How does ~~she~~ *they* act?
Michelle Obama	Forme- 1st lady	Kind, bold Confedent!
My mom	Orginiser	Kind, funny Amazing

Call Log

Haha!

Pay attention to how all these women act when they perform their roles. Do they:

✦ look people in the eye and speak firmly and clearly?

✦ use their hands or facial expressions for emphasis when they talk?

✦ make decisions for large groups of people?

✦ remind you of values in the Girl Scout Law? Are they honest and fair, friendly and helpful, considerate and caring, or … ?

Good leaders tend to do all these things, too. Which of them do you do? Which might you want to practice more?

Being a casting director forces you to observe people more closely than you ever have before. What do you notice about the women in your log that you hadn't noticed before? In what new ways are you now appreciating them?

Is this a role you would like to try? Why or why not?	What value(s) of the Girl Scout Law does she express in her role(s)?
be confedient	
Fun + orginised	

Word Play

"Cold reading" is reading aloud from a script without studying it ahead of time.

"Sight-reading" is playing music you've never seen before.

Sometimes a cold reading or a sight-reading is the only chance performers get to audition. *Yikes!*

Some performers practice cold reading and sight-reading to keep in shape. They open any new script or sheet music to a page, scan it quickly, and then perform!

This kind of practice can help *you*, too. When you are in the role of a friend, is there ever something that feels hard to say? How about when you are in the role of a leader and want to talk about a decision you've made? Practice what you want to say! Rehearse in front of a family member or someone else you trust—or just by yourself! When the real time comes, you'll be all warmed up and ready to go! **You'll be confident!**

Go Loosey-Goosey!

Acting Tip:

Here's an exercise actors use when they get stuck on something and feel frustrated. It can get you unstuck, too, in just 1 minute!

1. Stand with your feet planted a foot or so apart, then shake, rattle, and roll your arms, legs, hips, and head. Jump up and down.

2. Roar like a lion, whinny like a horse, and make other animal sounds.

3. Go wild for a few more seconds, then stop.

4. Breathe in and out, slowly and calmly. Now, how do you feel? Hopefully, you'll feel relaxed or invigorated, and ready to give whatever you're stuck on another try.

"Role Model" Dolls

Here's a fun way to use buttons and pipe cleaners to make teeny-tiny dolls to represent the roles of women and girls you know.

MATERIALS

- Two pipe cleaners
- One large button
- Yarn in colors of your choice
- Glue
- Felt or other material of your choice to make the eyes, nose, and mouth

1 Pull one pipe cleaner through the holes in the button.

2 Make a body for the doll by twisting the pipe cleaner a few times, leaving the ends straight to be the legs.

3 To make arms, twist a smaller piece of the second pipe cleaner right under the button.

4 Wrap yarn tightly around the button. Once it's covered, move down and wrap it around the rest of the body. If you have an extra bit of pipe cleaner, use it to pad out the body.

5 Wrap another color of yarn around your doll to make pants and a top, or other clothes. Then tie or glue the ends of the yarn to stop them from unraveling.

6 Glue on the eyes, nose, and mouth with materials of your choice. Finish by gluing bits of thread on the head for hair.

7 Bend and twist your doll into whatever pose you like.

Enjoy!

All-My-Roles Paper Dolls

Student, daughter, Girl Scout, singer, leader. . . . You have so many roles! You can have fun making paper dolls and decorating them to represent all your roles.

MATERIALS

- Paper
- Crayons or colored markers or pencils
- Bits of fabric, sequins, and other odds and ends to decorate
- Scissors

1 Start with a sheet of white paper and fold it over and over, like a fan.

2 Then draw a doll on the top of the folded paper. Be sure the doll's arms reach all the way to the sides of the paper.

3 Next, cut out your doll but not the sides! Open up the string of dolls. They'll look like they're holding hands.

4 Decorate them to represent all your many roles!

{ Draw what you think happens next }

EVERY WEEK THERE'S A SURPRISE. SO LET ME INTRODUCE MS. SHEILA BROOKS, A RETIRED JUDGE AND

THE FIFTH MEMBER OF YOUR TEAM!

TURN TO PAGE 26 TO SEE THE NEXT CHALLENGE!

A Dancer Who Dazzles

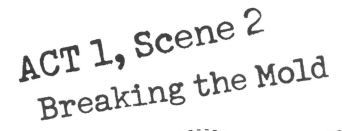

Bennaldra "Benny" Williams performs for a modern dance company in Brooklyn, New York.

The company's dancers are all black women. Some are tall, some are short, some are thin, and some aren't. They also range in skin tone from dark to caramel to light. Together this dance company shows that neither beauty nor talent are limited to one size, shape, or color.

Benny, for example, who is 5 feet 1 inch tall, dazzles with her speed and explosive leaps and turns. Taller dancers move across the stage in a flowing, expansive manner. Other dancers are experts at "floor work," the close-to-the-ground moves that require dancers to work with—and against—the force of gravity. "This variety within the group helps everyone," Benny says. "It gives us others to learn from."

Benny was a Girl Scout growing up in Birmingham, Alabama. When she was 12, she auditioned for a special school for the arts. She had only started dance lessons two months before.

At the tryout, the teacher asked dancers to perform ballet steps with French names like "double *pirouette*," which means "two turns," a "*pas de bourree*," or quick steps, and a "*tour jeté*," or a turning leap through the air. "I was like, oh, my gosh. I can't do any of this. I was freaking out," Benny says.

Then she remembered some advice her mother had given her before the audition: *Do the best that you can do*. "That kept me going," Benny recalls. And it has to this day.

Think Again: Take 2!

A *stereotype* is an overly simple view of someone or a group of people, such as saying, "short girls aren't good at basketball." If you ever find yourself casting people in certain roles without thinking about them as individuals first, you might be using a stereotype.

5'3"

By the way, did you know that **Debbie Black**, who is just 5 feet 3 inches tall, played professional basketball for 18 seasons? She was the shortest player in the Women's National Basketball Association league, yet she was named the WNBA's Defensive Player of the Year in 2001.

Movies, TV shows, and even advertisements might cause you to think in stereotypes. For instance, if all the dancers shown in movies, on TV, and in magazines looked the same—all tall and thin, for example—some people might believe that only people who looked that way could be dancers. Stereotypes can prevent people from playing all the wonderful roles that life offers!

When in your life have you seen people thinking in stereotypes? How could the world be better if people didn't think that way? Over a few days or a week or two, keep track of any stereotypes you find around you.

{ Draw what you think happens next }

Stereotype Tracker

Stereotype	Where I found it	What I could do to stop it	How what I could do would make the world better

TURN TO PAGE 34 TO SEE THE NEXT CHALLENGE!

CALL!

GOOD NEWS!

ACT 1, Scene 3
"The Callback"

Talk About Roles

After an audition, some actors are asked to a "callback." That's a second audition. It's a chance for the director to take a closer look before she decides who's best for the part.

Try this!

Choose a woman from your Casting Call Log that you'd like to know better.
Ask your parent or guardian to approve your choice and help you arrange a
talk or get-together so you can ask her about all the roles she plays—
and has played—in her life. Let her know that you're on this aMUSEing journey
exploring all the roles women play in your life and your community.

Here are some questions you might ask:

What are the roles that
you play in your life today—
at your job, in your family,
as a volunteer?

What role did you take on
at some point in your life that you never
really expected to have?

What did you
learn from it?

Where did it lead you next?

Did you ever have to
give up on a role you wanted and
try something else?

Has anything stopped you
from playing any of your roles?

Have you ever
had to confront a stereotype?
If so, what happened?

Are there women who
paved the way for you in your roles?
Who are they, and what have
you learned from them?

What stereotypes do you think girls
my age face in the world today?

What can we do
about stereotypes?

What other roles do you hope to try
at some point?

What did you want to be
when you were my age?

Also ask the woman you chose to talk to which qualities and values in the Girl Scout Law are most important in her roles, and why they're important to her.

Check the ones she thinks are key, and write her reason or reasons next to it.

☐ Honest ....

☐ Fair ....

☐ Friendly ....

☐ Helpful ....

☐ Considerate ....

☐ Caring ....

☐ Courageous ....

☐ Strong ....

☐ Responsible for what I say and do ....

☐ Respect myself and others ....

☐ Respect authority ....

☐ Use resources wisely ....

☐ Make the world a better place ....

If you can, record your interview with the woman or take a photo of the two of you together, or make a drawing and paste it here.

Now take time to think about what you learned during the callback. Share your thoughts here.

What surprised you most about your role model and her roles?

....
....

What values and qualities do you share with her?

....
....

How do you think she acts as a leader in or through her roles?

....
....

What surprised you most about your role model and her roles?

....
....

How would you like to be more like her?

....
....

What did you learn about stereotypes from her?

....
....

Training Pretend Patients

Carol Fleishman teaches people how to fake colds, coughs, backaches, and other ailments—all for a good cause. She trains people to play the role of patients, so that medical students can become better doctors.

Here's how it works: Medical students learn a lot from their books and their classes, but they also need to practice talking with and examining real people. That's where Carol comes in.

She trains people to pretend to be patients. "I teach them how to act. If their back is hurting, how should they hold their bodies? How should they react when a 'sore' place is touched? What should their facial expression be? How would they talk?"

Carol works for the Maine Medical Center, a teaching hospital in Portland, Maine. The first programs to use role-playing for teaching and testing medical students started about 45 years ago and are now in use at medical schools around the nation.

Role players are also used to train other medical professionals, including nurses, pharmacists, and current doctors. They help train lawyers, too, by pretending to be someone who needs assistance with a legal issue. Some role players are "mystery shoppers." They go into businesses, such as stores and restaurants, to check out how well salesclerks and other employees treat their customers.

Who does Carol hire to play patients? Sometimes she hires actors, but mostly she hires everyday people, including children and teens. The children usually pretend they are seeing the doctor for a checkup or because they have a cold, cough, asthma, or leg pains. "We use babies, too," Carol adds, "but the babies have an easy job of being themselves!"

A Longtime Girl Scout Role

A long-standing role in Girl Scouts is that of the Honorary National President. It's a tradition that dates back to 1917. The First Lady of the United States usually fills this role.

Edith B. Wilson (pictured) was the first U.S. First Lady to take on the role. Since then, each First Lady has served in the post. So, today, in addition to her roles as First Lady, mom, leader in the fight against childhood obesity, and gardener, Michelle Obama has a key role in Girl Scouts! What values of the Girl Scout Law do you think she cherishes most?

New Roles, New Records

As a young girl, **Lynne Cox** loved swimming and dreamed of competing in the Olympics. She joined a swim team and practiced up to three hours a day. But no matter how long she trained or how hard she tried, she was a slow swimmer.

Me!

FOR THE NEXT CHALLENGE, THE TEAM GOES TO THE CITY LIBRARY . . .

FIND THE BOOK WITH THIS DEWEY DECIMAL NUMBER, GO TO PAGE 127, AND NAME WHAT'S ON IT.

CIRCULATION DESK

NONFICTION BOOKS

I FOUND IT! IT'S A BOOK ABOUT THE STARS.

THEY OPEN THE BOOK TO PAGE 127 AND FIND . . .

A STAR CHART!

Then one day at a practice, when she was 8 years old, her teammates got so cold that they all got out of the pool. Lynne kept swimming. She found that the longer she swam in the cold water, the warmer she felt. She discovered a new role for herself: long-distance, cold-water swimmer!

The mother of a teammate predicted that Lynne would one day swim the English Channel. Lynne took the prediction seriously. When she was 15, she swam across the channel from England to France, a distance of 21 miles. She swam it in 9 hours and 57 minutes—fast enough to break both the women's *and* men's records.

Since then, Lynne has broken records all around the world. She has also tried on yet another role, that of best-selling author. In her books, she tells stories about her swimming encounters with penguins, dolphins, whales, and sharks, and about her other adventures in the ocean and on land.

Lynne's latest big swim traced the route of the first Arctic explorer to make it through the Northwest Passage, from Greenland to Alaska.

Lynne first learned about the explorer through stories a Norwegian friend told her nearly 40 years ago, as she trained to swim the English Channel.

"Whether you're young or old, what you say to people can inspire them," Lynne says.

That's why it's so important to tell—and to listen to—stories. You never know what new role they might inspire!

{ Draw what you think happens next }

HEY! IT LOOKS LIKE AN ANIMAL!

OH, THAT'S CAMELOPARDALIS! IT'S A CONSTELLATION. ITS NAME REALLY MEANS "GIRAFFE" IN LATIN. ISN'T THAT WILD?

DON'T ACT SO SURPRISED THAT I KNOW THAT! JUST BECAUSE I LOVE MOVIE STARS DOESN'T MEAN I CAN'T LOVE THE ONES IN THE SKY, TOO!

TURN TO PAGE 42 TO SEE THE NEXT CHALLENGE!

ACT 2, Scene 1
Turning Acting into Action

The best stories sweep you away to another world. You get caught up in the action, you start to care about the characters, and you wonder what they'll do next. You laugh, cry, gasp, and smile, as if the events in the story are real. A good story has that much power!

Really good stories have a lot in common. What happens in them usually follows a pattern. For instance, often the main character—the heroine—faces various challenges and finds herself in situations that test her inner strength.

Remember when Lynne Cox stayed in the pool after her teammates got out because they were cold? Look where that led her. That's quite a story!

But what if people had allowed stereotypes to limit their vision and instead told Lynne, "You're too young to swim the English Channel," or "You're a girl, you can't do that!" or "You're too slow to ever be an athlete"? And what if she had believed them? Then she might not have taken on her new role . . . and her story certainly would be different!

Production:

Director:

Scene: Date:

Take:

Storytelling with a Purpose

SPEAK OUT!

Speaking out against stereotypes is one way to try to stop them.

As a step toward the Speak Out! award, you and your sister Juniors will create a story about why it's important for people to support women and girls in trying out new roles. Your story will show why it's important not to limit your thinking about all the roles people can play in life.

Great actors and storytellers capture their audiences' attention when they tell their stories—and you can, too! You'll tell your story to an audience with the aim of educating and inspiring them about stereotypes. If you can hold your audience's attention, you'll have the best chance of getting your message across!

So give these tips and techniques a try:

Characters Who Count

When telling your story, present your main character—the heroine—as realistically as you can. She doesn't have to be perfect. That way, people will root for her in whatever roles she chooses to take on.

Conflict

Suppose you want to do something and a friend wants to do something else. That's a conflict. Conflict can keep people interested in your story. It may even get them thinking about trying on a new role as peacemaker!

HA!

HA!

HUMOR! That's a good way to keep people listening. Do you know any jokes?

KNOCK, KNOCK!

Who's there?

DEZ!

Dez who?

Dez anybody know what time it is?

GOOD ONE!

haha

Cliff-Hanger

Cliff-hanger comes from the image of someone dangling from a cliff, maybe just by her fingertips. You don't know how long she's going to be able to hang on. In stories, cliff-hangers usually come at the end of a chapter or an act. On the Internet, you might have to click to find out what happens next! On TV, cliff-hangers make you want to tune in to the next episode or season. When telling your story, create your own cliff-hanger—give a nice pause before you say (or show) whether your heroine will overcome her challenge.

Ticking Clock

Suppose a character is racing to put clues together before her archenemy does, or she's rushing to the airport to stop the villain's plane from taking off. That's a ticking clock. It's a storytelling device that builds tension. When you tell your story, see if you can build in a "will she make it in time?" scene about your heroine as she reaches for her new role.

39

Stories Circle the Globe!

Stories have been around in so many forms for thousands of years. They've been told with puppets and in plays, through dance and song. Even large paintings, like the murals you might see on the sides of buildings, tell stories.

Today, people also tell stories in many newer ways, such as posting photos and videos on the Internet. **Muse about the many storytelling forms as you pick a way to tell your story.**

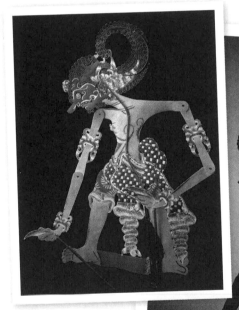

In Javanese shadow plays, stick puppets cast shadows on a screen. The puppeteer in these plays is very busy. That's because one puppeteer controls all the puppets' movements and their voices, and the shows last from dusk to dawn. **Imagine working a puppet all night long!**

In Japan, 2- to 4-foot-tall puppets with wooden heads are called Bunraku puppets. The puppeteers are right on stage, but they're hard to see because **they dress all in black to blend into the background.**

Vietnamese water puppet shows were first performed in rice paddies. Now they're performed on a water-filled stage, and **the puppets look like they're dancing on the water.** The puppeteers are behind a screen. They use large rods hidden under the water to make the puppets move.

Artist Julie Taymor, who lives in New York, studied many puppet styles before she created the life-size animal puppets in the hit Broadway show "The Lion King." Her giraffes, wildebeests, and other animal puppets are operated by actors who are inside the puppets and can be seen by the audience. **What a role for the puppeteers, who sing and dance!**

"Daisy" Gordon Low: Playwright and Star

Juliette "Daisy" Gordon Low loved to act and write plays. She gave amusing names to the characters she created. She loved fancy costumes, and had a talent for memorizing lines. When she was growing up, her family spent summers at her Aunt Eliza's house at Etowah Cliffs, in Cartersville, Georgia. As many as 20 cousins, along with aunts and uncles, would gather there. Daisy and the other children performed their plays for the grown-ups. After all, they didn't have YouTube, computer games, or Wii for entertainment. Movies and TV hadn't even been invented!

So the children made up plays, and played all the roles. They based some plays on old family tales. For others, they chose the life of Mary, Queen of Scots (Daisy's family was Scottish), and stories from the Civil War (Daisy was a little girl during that war). Everyone agreed that Daisy was the most fun to watch in the plays.

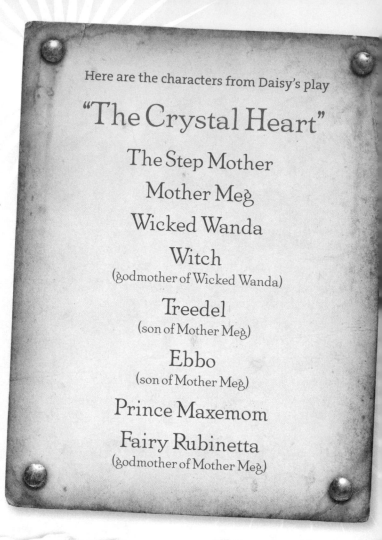

Here are the characters from Daisy's play

"The Crystal Heart"

The Step Mother

Mother Meg

Wicked Wanda

Witch
(godmother of Wicked Wanda)

Treedel
(son of Mother Meg)

Ebbo
(son of Mother Meg)

Prince Maxemom

Fairy Rubinetta
(godmother of Mother Meg)

YOUR NEXT CHALLENGE IS THIS SIDEWALK! DRAW SOMETHING YOU CAN SEE RIGHT HERE ON THIS BLOCK!

WOW! THESE ARE SO BEAUTIFUL—BUT THEY MUST TAKE HOURS!

WE'VE BEEN OUT HERE SINCE DAWN! I WISH I'D BROUGHT KNEE PADS!

I THINK I CAN MAKE A CHALK DRAWING REALLY FAST!

Have some fun making up a story that uses Daisy's characters.

What roles will they play? What stereotypes will they bust? What storytelling techniques will you use?

....

....

....

....

....

....

....

....

....

....

OM-I-GOSH, SUN-AH! IT LOOKS JUST LIKE THE SHADOW OF THE PARKING METER! WHAT A NEAT TRICK!

IT'S CALLED TROMPE L'OEIL. THAT MEANS "TRICK OF THE EYE," AND IT REALLY DOES . . .

TRICK THE EYE!

FANTASTIC! I CAN'T BELIEVE HOW FAST YOU DID IT!

THE TOUGHER THE CHALLENGE, THE BETTER MY IMAGINATION WORKS!

{ Draw what you think happens next }

TURN TO PAGE 54 TO SEE THE NEXT CHALLENGE!

ACT 2, Scene 2
Getting in on the Action

Your Heart. Your Art. Your Part

Find your talent or what you love to do—that's what's in **your heart.** Next, find a creative way that you can use what you love to do—that's **your art.** Then see what role you can play when you and your Junior team get together to tell a story about stereotypes—that's **your part!** And remember that not all actors, musicians, photographers, painters, or directors look or act the same, so you can take on whatever roles you want.

If you like to...	Then you might try...	Your role could be...
Play an instrument	Concert, musical theater, TV show, movie, dance, video	Musician (saxophonist, guitarist, pianist, violinist, percussionist), or ....
Listen to music	Musical theater, concert, video, TV show, movie	Musical director, disc jockey, or ....
Doodle	Mural, painting, animation, Web-page design, children's stories, stage/set design	Painter, animator, designer, illustrator, or ....
Put together unique outfits or help others	Plays, musical theater, video, TV shows, movie	Costume designer, or ....
Observe everything around you	Photography, video, TV show, movie, animation	Photographer, videographer, muralist, writer, or ....
Move	Musical theater, dance, sports	Dancer, choreographer, athlete, coach, or ....
Tell jokes and make people laugh	TV or funny play, musical theater, comedy show, video	Gag writer, comic actor, or ....
Think up stories and scenes	Plays, movie, TV show	Writer, director, or ....
Keep everything and everyone organized	Directing or managing any kind of storytelling	Director, production manager, stage manager
Have fun with color and/or shapes	Mural, painting, animation, photography, video, Web-page design, scrapbooking	Muralist, painter, animator, photographer, videographer, designer, scrapbooker
People watch	Plays, movie, TV show	Writer, director, casting director
Speak in public	Plays, musical theater, video, TV show, movie, animation	Actor
Sing	Musical theater, TV show, movie, animation	Singer
Listen in on conversations	Plays, musical theater, TV show, movie	Writer, director, casting director
Imagine and dream	Anything!	Writer, director, painter, animator, videographer, actor, scrapbooker

Project Toolbox

Creative people need tools when they create—tools they hold in their hands and tools that get their imagination going. Remember, not everyone can sing as well as Beyoncé, or write as well as J.K. Rowling, but that doesn't mean they're not creative.

Check the qualities you think it takes to be a creative person or problem solver:

☐ Ideas

☐ Inspiration

☐ Guts

☐ Originality

☐ Honesty

☐ Talent

☐ Creativity

☐ Stick-to-itiveness

☐ Passion

☐ Openness to mentors

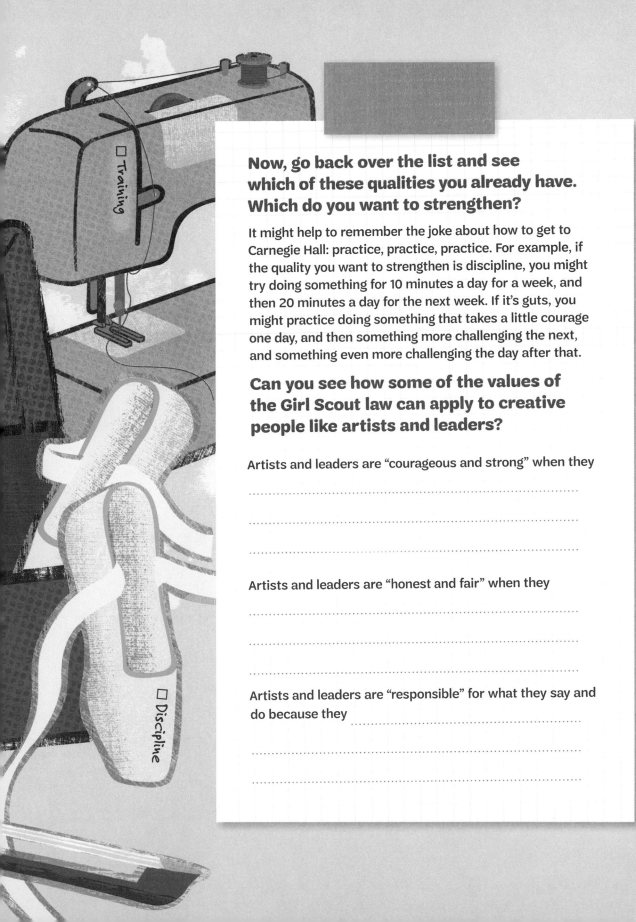

□ Training

□ Discipline

Now, go back over the list and see which of these qualities you already have. Which do you want to strengthen?

It might help to remember the joke about how to get to Carnegie Hall: practice, practice, practice. For example, if the quality you want to strengthen is discipline, you might try doing something for 10 minutes a day for a week, and then 20 minutes a day for the next week. If it's guts, you might practice doing something that takes a little courage one day, and then something more challenging the next, and something even more challenging the day after that.

Can you see how some of the values of the Girl Scout law can apply to creative people like artists and leaders?

Artists and leaders are "courageous and strong" when they

....

....

....

Artists and leaders are "honest and fair" when they

....

....

....

Artists and leaders are "responsible" for what they say and do because they ....

....

....

Give a Picture a New Story

You've heard the phrase "Every picture tells a story."

Find a family photo that you're in. Put yourself in the role of someone else in the photo and tell a little story from that other person's point of view. Be as realistic as you want, as imaginative as you can be, or as silly as you feel like. Try to bust some stereotypes in your story, too! Paste the photo or draw a copy of it here, and then write your story:

Daisy and Her Stories

Juliette "Daisy" Gordon Low enjoyed telling aMUSE-ing stories and jokes at parties and other gatherings.

Storytelling helped Daisy because she was nearly deaf. She found that when she told funny stories, she was able to put herself and others at ease—because she didn't have to struggle to understand what was said, and her audience didn't have to wonder whether she was hearing them. When Daisy lived in England, one of her neighbors was the famous storyteller Rudyard Kipling, the author of *The Jungle Book*. He created the character Rikki-Tikki-Tavi, the brave mongoose who fights a big, mean cobra. Kipling and Daisy became good friends. What kind of stories do you and your friends tell when you get together?

So Many Ways to Bust Stereotypes!

Bethany Hamilton won her first surfing competition when she was just 8 years old. By the time she was a teenager, she was a well-known surfer.

Then, on October 31, 2003, her world changed. A tiger shark attacked 13-year-old Bethany when she was surfing near the Hawaiian island of Kauai. The 14-foot shark tore off most of her left arm.

Despite her injury, Bethany was determined to return to surfing. Just one month after the attack, she was back on her board. Later that year, she published her autobiography. In 2011, more people learned about Bethany's inspiring story when a successful movie—*Soul Surfer*—was made out of her first book.

By sharing her experiences, Bethany has changed the way people view female athletes and those who are differently abled.

"People I don't even know come up to me," she writes. "I guess they see me as a symbol of courage and inspiration. One thing hasn't changed, and that's how I feel when I'm riding a wave. It's like, I'm still here."

When **Ellen Ochoa** was in high school in the early 1970s, girls were not always encouraged to succeed in math and science. But Ellen was good at those subjects, and she had a calculus teacher who encouraged her.

When she went to college, however, one of her professors told her that engineering was too difficult for women. She proved that professor wrong in 1991, when she was selected by the National Aeronautics and Space Administration (NASA) as the world's first Hispanic female astronaut!

Just two years later, Ellen Ochoa became the first Hispanic woman to go into space. And today, she has logged more than 1,000 hours in space!

Mitali Perkins grew up in California, where she often felt caught between two worlds—her traditional Bengali family and the American suburbs. She loved to read, but she had a hard time finding books that talked about people who were having experiences like hers.

As a writer, she was able to change that. Her first book, *The Not-So-Star-Spangled Life of Sunita Sen*, told the story of a California middle-schooler and her traditional Indian family.

Mitali wants to get more people challenging the stereotypes that are often associated with different cultures. "Let the stories come," she writes. "The more novels about a diversity of characters written by a diversity of authors and consumed by a diversity of readers, the better."

Flip and Trade for More Ideas!

Bethany Hamilton didn't let a terrible accident affect what she could do in the sport of surfing. Ellen Ochoa didn't let someone's opinion about girls' math skills keep her from being an astronaut. Mitali Perkins didn't let the fact that she couldn't find books that reflected her cultural experiences stop her from writing her own.

What stereotypes would you like to see change so women and girls and ANYONE can try on whatever roles they want?

Trade ideas with your Junior friends! The more ideas you trade, the more ideas you'll have for your Speak Out story. Consider getting started by creating cards to share that will help others get out of the habit of using stereotypes.

- First, get a stack of blank index cards or cut small pieces of paper into squares or rectangles.

- Then, draw a picture of a person who is stereotyped on one side of the card. For example, maybe it's a girl with a speech balloon saying, "Math is hard."

- Flip the card over and on the other side, draw a picture of the stereotype BUSTED! For example, you could draw a girl with a speech balloon that says, "Math might be hard for some people, but I'm really good at it!"

For more fun, make extra copies of your cards to trade with your friends and create your own Stereotype Busting Card Pack.

Thinking Like a Storyteller

When creating a story, think like a storyteller. Storytellers often start with an interesting heroine, so why don't you? What will you call her? How does she act? What does she do? It's all up to you!

My heroine's name is ....

She lives in ....

She's worried about this kind of stereotype; ....

She's worried about it because ....

Her best friend is ....

She likes to wear ....

Her favorite book/TV show/hobby is ....

She wishes for ....

SPEAK OUT

Choosing Your Audience

Every story needs an audience. You want people to get to know your heroine, laugh at her jokes, and root for her when she takes on stereotypes and faces other challenges. You want your story to educate and inspire.

So, who's your audience? Well, who cares about the stereotypes you care about? Who can change those stereotypes? They might be little kids or families. They might be students in your class or from another school, or people you don't know yet. Who will join you in busting stereotypes? That's your audience!

Getting Your Audience on Its Feet

Once you've told your story, you want to get your audience on its feet and ready to take action! What do you want people to say or do?

You want them to join you in dealing with roles and stereotypes differently, right? So you might ask them to promise to be on the lookout for stereotyping in their own lives—and to not give in to it. You might ask them to support a woman or girl who's trying on a challenging new role—or even to try on new roles themselves.

That's inspiring others. And when you inspire others, you make change! That's being a great storyteller and a Girl Scout! And that's being a leader, too! Wow! Look at all the roles you're playing!

Break a leg, Dez! That means "GOOD LUCK."

Some people think "break a leg" comes from the tradition of actors taking a bow. Bowing had them "breaking" the line of their leg.

At least that's one explanation.

Maybe I'll have really good luck in telling my story and break all four of my legs!

Green Goddess Dip and Veggies

This healthful, energizing snack is yummy enough to turn the Muses green with envy.

NEXT, THE TEAM BOARDS A CITY BUS . . .

AND ONE OF THEM MUST PRETEND TO BE AN ENTERTAINING ANNOUNCER FOR A TOUR OF THE CITY . . .

I KNOW! I'M A TOTAL FOODIE. I CAN DO A FOOD LOVER'S TOUR!

WELCOME TO TODAY'S FOOD LOVERS' TOUR OF OUR FAIR CITY. IF YOU'RE HUNGRY, YOU'RE ON THE RIGHT BUS!

ON YOUR RIGHT IS BEST BURGERS EVER, A BURGER JOINT WITH ATTITUDE. YOU MIGHT EVEN SPOT OUR MAYOR, MIRACLE GONZALES, IN THERE. SHE LIKES HERS WITH EXTRA PICKLES!

Ingredients:

½ cup fresh mint
½ cup fresh parsley
½ cup fresh basil
2 garlic cloves, chopped
2 scallions/green onions sliced
1½ tablespoons lemon juice

pinch of salt (optional)
½ cup olive oil
½ cup crumbled feta cheese
½ cup plain Greek yogurt
raw chopped vegetables for dipping

Place mint, parsley, basil, garlic, scallions, and lemon juice in a food processor or blender and process until the ingredients are finely chopped.

Add olive oil and continue to process the mixture until combined well. Add feta and yogurt, and process until smooth. Taste dip and add a pinch of salt, if you like. If you add salt, be sure to process the mixture again!

Serve immediately with your choice of fresh vegetables, like broccoli and cauliflower florets, celery and carrot sticks, and red, green, or yellow bell peppers. Or cover and refrigerate until ready to serve.

Acting Tip:

Shake it up!

Tongue twisters are a traditional training technique for actors. Singers and storytellers also sometimes say something simple and silly several times swiftly to sharpen their speech.

Give it a try with this one:

Go like gangbusters and give girls the get-up-and-go to gallop through this glorious world with gumption, grabbing any great roles that grab them.

Then try it when you ask your audience to pledge to support women and girls in their choice of roles. Be sure to ask them to say it as fast as possible!

{ Draw what you think happens next }

THERE'S SWEET SARAH'S BAKERY. THEIR CINNAMON ROLLS ARE THE BEST. WE HEAR BOBBY FLAY IS COMING SOON FOR A "THROWDOWN"!

ARACELI HAS EVERYONE'S ATTENTION, AND PASSENGERS BEGIN ASKING HER WHERE THE TOUR WILL BE STOPPING TO EAT.

TURN TO PAGE 60 TO SEE THE NEXT CHALLENGE!

ACT 3, Scene 1

The Role of a Lifetime, Starring…YOU!

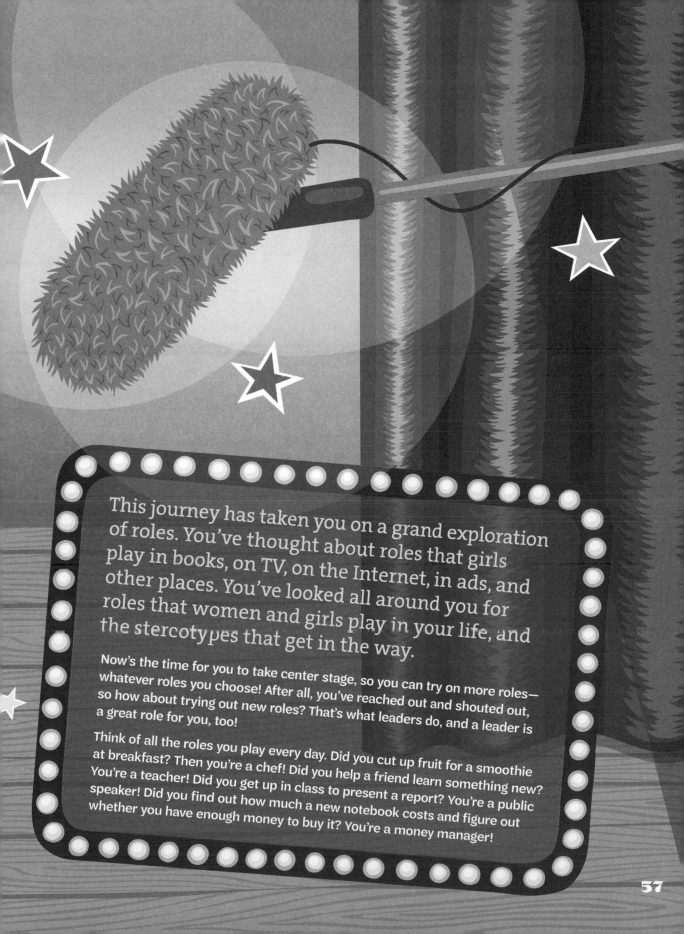

This journey has taken you on a grand exploration of roles. You've thought about roles that girls play in books, on TV, on the Internet, in ads, and other places. You've looked all around you for roles that women and girls play in your life, and the stereotypes that get in the way.

Now's the time for you to take center stage, so you can try on more roles—whatever roles you choose! After all, you've reached out and shouted out, so how about trying out new roles? That's what leaders do, and a leader is a great role for you, too!

Think of all the roles you play every day. Did you cut up fruit for a smoothie at breakfast? Then you're a chef! Did you help a friend learn something new? You're a teacher! Did you get up in class to present a report? You're a public speaker! Did you find out how much a new notebook costs and figure out whether you have enough money to buy it? You're a money manager!

My "Role Call" Log

Try this! Keep track of all the roles you play for a few days or a week.

Then think about the skills and traits you use when you perform the roles. And think about how performing those roles makes you feel. You might feel creative or practical in the role of a chef. Or smart and useful in the role of a teacher. Does performing one role well make you confident that you can take on others, too?

Funny Faces!

Acting Tip:

When actors want to "loosen up" or get the jitters out before a show, they sometimes make funny faces. Try it when you want to warm up before presenting to a group.

Open your mouth as wide as you can to form a big "O." Then cover your teeth with your lips and make a smaller "O."

Next, scrunch up your face. Shut your eyes tight, purse your lips together, and furrow your brow. Hold for a few seconds, then relax.

Repeat it a few times.

How do you feel? Any different than before? Are the muscles in your face warmed up? Are you relaxed and ready to go?

Role	Skills and traits the role takes	How does the role make you feel?	How close is this role to the real you?

Trading Roles

TRY OUT!

What roles make you feel like an expert?

Are you a math whiz, a spelling champ, or a skateboard hotdog? Have you ever taught someone how to do what you can do well, and felt great about it?

When you're in the role of teacher, think about how you act. Are you patient and kind? Do you break things down so your student will understand them better? Do you slow down and repeat things when your student is not getting them? Do you encourage her and let her know that she can do it?

Try these same traits on yourself when you're learning something new or challenging! Suppose you get frustrated trying to learn a new dance or a new computer game. Be patient with yourself. Break the steps down into small parts so they're easier to learn. **Ask for help! Tell yourself you can do it, and keep at it until you can!**

Roles I tried	How it went	What I learned	What I might try next time

{ Draw what you think happens next }

TURN TO PAGE 74 TO SEE WHAT HAPPENS NEXT!

Confident, Stylish, and Goofy!

TV chef and co-host

Carla Hall definitely

knows how to be herself!

When growing up, Carla studied acting and performed in plays. That gave her the confidence to be herself.

Being in theater meant doing a lot of acting exercises, she recalls. "It was about being free, and saying and doing whatever you want," she says. "It was about 'dare to be you, dare to be different.' A lot of people see that as kooky. But for me, it's actually about confidence. I'm OK with people calling me goofy because to me, it's synonymous with confidence."

Competing on a reality TV show, Carla showed confidence—and spirit, and spunk. She told others to "feel the love" in her food, and she shouted out, "Hootie-hoo!" whenever she felt like it.

Carla got her start with food as a Girl Scout in Tennessee. Girl Scouting showed her that the outdoors and food go together as naturally as peanut butter and jelly—or green eggs and ham! Carla whipped up green eggs and ham when she competed on TV. Pureed spinach made the eggs green, and she served them with green tomato salsa.

In her mid-20s, Carla worked as a model in Paris. But she liked cooking so much that she eventually went to cooking school. The first time she put on an official chef's coat, she noticed how she felt. "It was like, 'Oh, it's serious, I'm really doing this.' That felt really good. It was a rite of passage for me," she says.

That's definitely a case of inner confidence shaping outer style and outer style supporting inner confidence!

When Carla made it to the finale of the competition, the stakes got higher, and for a moment she lost sight of who she is as a chef. She ended up cooking beef in a way she'd never tried before—the way her sous-chef wanted her to cook it. That dish cost Carla the win, but it taught her an important lesson: Always have the confidence to do things your way!

Show-Stopping Snacks

Food that's good for you can also be aMUSE-ing—especially if it's an amuse-bouche. That's a French term, and you say it like this:

uh-MYUZ-boosh.

It means an amusement ("amuse") for the mouth ("bouche")—a small bite of food that's eaten before a meal, like an appetizer.

Here are Carla Hall's ideas for simple, healthful *amuses-bouche:*

Clear chicken broth with vegetables and teeny-tiny noodles. Use store-bought or homemade chicken broth; onions and carrots chopped into a fine dice; and small noodles, such as little stars or another shape. Cook the noodles and warm up the broth with the veggies. Serve them together in a small cup, such as one used for espresso.

Mushroom cap "pizzas." Remove the stems from washed white mushrooms and sprinkle the caps with shredded mozzarella cheese, diced roasted tomatoes, and fresh basil or oregano. Pop them in a 350-degree oven until the cheese melts.

Fresh figs stuffed with goat cheese and drizzled with apple- or white grape-juice reduction. Halve the figs, and stuff with a teaspoonful of cheese. Make the reduction using a can of frozen juice concentrate boiled over high heat for about 10 minutes, until it thickens. Be sure it cools thoroughly before you drizzle it. You can also top the stuffed figs with roasted, chopped almonds.

Ask an adult to help you with these recipes.

Dressing the Part

Costume designers dress the actors in plays, TV shows, and movies. The clothes an actor wears can tell the audience a lot about the character being portrayed.

Costumes also help actors play their roles. An actress will walk and act differently when she's wearing an evening gown and dressy shoes than when she's in jeans and has a backpack slung over her shoulder.

An actress playing a character who lived in the past might wear a corset underneath her costume. A corset is a type of girdle that cinches in the waist to make it look tiny. But it also makes it hard to move—and even breathe!

"An actress wearing a corset realizes that her character can't do a lot of things that we take for granted," says **Angela Calin**, a costume and set designer who lives in southern California. "You can't run. You can't bend down to lace your boots. You can only sit in a certain position. So that helps the actress." And it tells the audience about the role of women during those times.

JAMES AND THE GIANT PEACH

GRASSHOPPER

LADY BUG

JANE GLA

To figure out what clothes a character needs, Angela first reads the script. That way she learns who the characters are, and where and when the play is set. Then she heads to the library to learn about the era, the setting, and the customs of people who lived then. She gets lots of ideas and inspiration from art books.

"The closer we get to today, the more information we have in different forms— magazines, newspapers, the Internet," she says. "But for times when there were no cameras, no photographs, you have to rely on artists who painted portraits."

Costume designers first draw or paint pictures of their costumes. Then they make patterns and sew the costumes. Sometimes they rent costumes from costume shops, borrow them from other theaters, prowl vintage or thrift shops, or shop for them—at the mall!

The Great Shakespeare

William Shakespeare's plays and poems are beloved around the world. During his lifetime, which was about 400 years ago, the roles of women were played by men.

Why? Because women were not allowed to act onstage. Thankfully, that's not the case anymore! In fact, today women can even be found playing the roles of men!

My Favorite "Costume"

What's your favorite outfit?

Is it something that makes you stand out from the crowd...

or blend in with

your friends?

Draw it, or describe it, or take a photo of yourself in it and paste it here.
Or make a video of yourself in it, maybe even acting the part in it!

Head First

Accessories—like hats, gloves, shoes, and jewelry—can be like costumes or props you put on and take off. Each one can reflect a different character or part of yourself. Each one can make you feel a different way. Have fun discovering new roles inspired by simple accessories!

Now, Head Out in a Hat or Scarf or . . .

Pick out a fun accessory. Make it something that catches people's attention. It could be a pair of sparkly tights, a pretty headband, an armload of colorful bracelets, or a hat—a snappy schoolboy cap, a chic beret, a big, floppy sun hat. Try it on and see how you look and how you feel. Wear your hat at a jaunty angle! Jangle your bracelets! Flick the scarf around your neck!

Do you feel pretty, daring, happy, proud, creative, courageous, or mysterious? Or something else? If you like how you feel, wear the accessory for a whole day. As you do, take note of how you feel when your friends notice the accessory. Is it hard or easy to be the center of attention? How do you feel when you take off the accessory? Does what you wear change you, or did you have that part of yourself inside you all along?

Record your experience!

Include a sketch of your accessory, or a picture of yourself wearing it.

The Power of Pins

Madeleine Albright was the first woman to serve as United States Secretary of State. That's an important role in the government. It's a job that requires meeting with leaders all around the world.

A Secretary of State, Madeleine wore fancy pins that gave her a boost in her role. The pins were a way of sending messages to the leaders she met. The kind of pin Madeleine wore depended on how things were going with the leader she happened to be meeting.

"If we were going to do happy things, or I was going to say something pleasant, I wore flowers and butterflies and balloons," Madeleine says. "On bad days, I wore various bugs and bees and weapons."

When Madeleine talked to world leaders about settling disputes, she often wore pins shaped like a dove, the universal symbol of peace. But if she felt that talks were moving too slowly, she took off the dove and wore a turtle or a snail. And when she felt frustrated, she pinned on a crab!

Most of Madeleine's pins were inexpensive. She often bought them at flea markets and airport gift shops. The pins can be fun and surprising, and that's a nice contrast to Madeleine's work, which is very serious and very hard. "It never hurts, I think, to do something slightly unexpected and have a sense of humor," she says.

Your Pin. Your Symbol.

Madeleine Albright wears a spider pin when she's feeling sneaky. Why?
The spider is the ancient symbol for patience and craftiness. What would Dez say about that?

Think of other symbols you know:
A dog can be a symbol for loyalty, a kitten for playfulness, a bluebird for happiness.

Create a symbol of your own and a pin or another piece of jewelry that uses it. Then wear it around. How do you feel with it on? How do people react?

The Girl Scout Pin

Since the Girl Scouts began, the trefoil has been its symbol of membership. Its three leaves stand for the three parts of the Girl Scout Promise.

The Girl Scout Traditional Membership Pin shows the eagle and shield of the Great Seal of the United States. The eagle symbolizes strength and victory. In its talons or claws, it holds arrows, a symbol of power, and an olive branch, a symbol of peace.

Today's Girl Scout Pin shows the faces of three girls—what a great way to symbolize this worldwide sisterhood!

Listening to Your Inner Critic

TRY OUT

Do you ever play the role of critic in your life?

Do you give yourself a thumbs-up when you do something that makes you feel good?

Maybe you scored a goal in soccer or accepted a compliment instead of brushing it off. Do you sometimes give a thumbs-down to something new or challenging even before you try it? Maybe you wanted to speak up, but didn't, when you heard a hurtful joke. Or maybe you wanted to try out, but didn't, for a bigger role in your school play.

Try this!

Name three things your inner critic might give a thumbs-up to that make you feel good.

1.

2.

3.

Name three things that your inner critic might give a thumbs-down to that you really want to try.

1.

2.

3.

How about turning that thumbs-down into a thumbs-up?

[Me] x 3

When someone praises you, you might brush it off, feeling you shouldn't gloat or feel prideful, or maybe you feel you don't deserve it. But some say it's good to do this instead:

Hear the praise, take it inside, and multiply it by three. Feel good about it!

Think about three things you're good at and that you have fun doing, and name them here:

1

2

3

Then do some math.
Multiply that compliment times three!

Word Play

"Leading role"

In acting, the "leading role" is the principal or starring part. Other arts have their own leading roles.

A **choreographer** is a leader in the world of dance.

A **conductor** is the leader of an orchestra.

THE GIRLS ARE STUNNED BY MS. BROOKS' GREAT PERFORMANCE. THEY RACE BACK TO THE STUDIO.

MS. BROOKS, YOU REALLY SAVED THE DAY! WE'RE LUCKY TO HAVE YOU ON OUR TEAM!

WAY TO GO! WHAT AN AMAZING WIN!

EACH OF US COMPLETED A CHALLENGE! AND WE ALL HAD TALENTS THE REST OF US NEVER IMAGINED!

A **network president** is a leader in television.

An **artistic director** is the leader of a theater.

Leaders in the arts are just like leaders in other fields. They:

- ✦ inspire and encourage
- ✦ set high standards
- ✦ communicate ideas
- ✦ stay open to the ideas of others

When you are a leader in your own life, you do these things, too.

At its best, art educates and inspires. When you're at your best, you can educate and inspire others, too.

Being an artist sometimes means saying or showing things not everyone will agree with or like. So being artistic and creative takes honesty and courage. Those are traits of good leaders, too.

Artists are leaders. Leaders are often artistic. Which are you? Or are you both?

{ Draw what you think happens next }

GIVE IT UP FOR OUR BIG WINNERS, THE AMAZING TEAM OF MEGAN, SUN-AH, ARABELA, ARACELI, AND MS. BROOKS. WHO KNEW THAT WOMAN HAD SUCH A SET OF PIPES?

AND WAIT 'TILL YOU SEE WHAT THEY WIN . . .

aMUSE
Award Tracker

To earn the award, you will:

✦ Keep a Casting Call Log of all the women and girls you encounter during a few days or a week.

✦ Choose one woman from the Casting Call Log and talk with her (do "The Callback") about the various roles she plays and has played in her life—even those she tried on for just a short time—to get a feel for what roles are possible for you!

Activity	Date	What I Learned
Keep a Casting Call Log (page 16–17)		
Talk About Roles ("The Callback") (pages 28–31)		

To earn the award, you will:

✦ Complete the three Speak Out! activities listed below to gain the skills to tell a story about stereotypes. Just look for the Speak Out! award icons.

✦ Join with your Junior friends to create and share a story in any medium you choose that gets people involved in challenging stereotypes. And if you can (for some *aMUSE*-ing bonus points!), check in with your audience later to see what impact your story had, and what they are now doing differently.

Activity	Date	What I Learned
Give a Picture a New Story (page 48)		
Flip and Trade for More Ideas! (page 51)		
Thinking Like a Storyteller (page 52)		

Action	Date	What I Learned
Find a stereotype that concerns you.		
Choose how to tell a story about it.		
Tell the story to an audience.		
Get your audience to join you in busting the stereotype and supporting women and girls in any roles they choose.		
BONUS: Check back on how your audience is doing.		

To earn the award, you will:

✦ Keep a "Role Call" Log of roles you play in your life for a few days or a week.

✦ Choose and complete two other Try Out! activities to give yourself the confidence to tackle even more roles. Look for the Try Out! icon.

✦ Then, as a team, form a Junior circle and take turns making a promise to keep trying out new roles.

Action	Date	What I Learned
My "Role Call" Log (page 58–59)		
Trading Roles (page 60–61)		
My Favorite "Costume" (page 66–67)		
Now, Head Out in a Hat or Scarf or . . . (page 69)		
Listening to Your Inner Critic (page 72)		
[Me] x 3 (page 73)		

✦ *Promise to keep trying out new roles.*

The Envelope, Please.

And the Winner Is . . .

Write your thoughts here:

You've probably watched actors in fancy clothes make speeches when they win awards for the roles they play. They thank all the people who helped them along the way, like their director, fellow actors, teachers, and family members.

Now it's time for your acceptance speech!

Think about all the things you've accomplished along this journey and all the people you've met along the way. Who would you like to thank—your Junior teammates, perhaps? Your audience? All the women you talked to along this journey?

MUSE-ing on Down the Road

You've reached out, you've spoken out, and you've tried out. You've seen how creative and powerful both roles and stories can be. Maybe you've found some new roles you want to play in your life. With all the new creativity you have, take time to think about all the ways you're a leader in every part of your life.

As you tried on new roles, what did you discover about yourself and the values you live by?

What did you enjoy most about connecting with others beyond your Junior group?

How did educating and inspiring others also educate and inspire you?

What would you like to inspire people to do next?

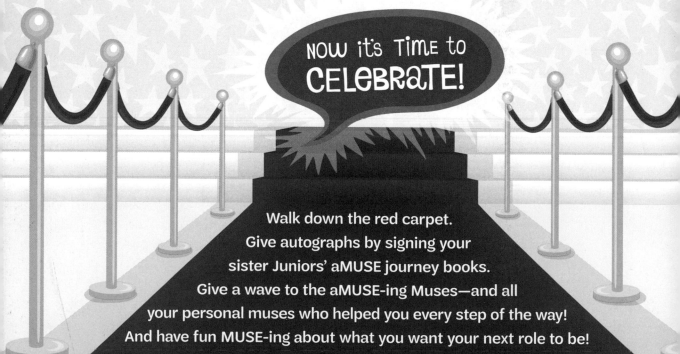

NOW it's TIME to CELEBRATE!

Walk down the red carpet.
Give autographs by signing your
sister Juniors' aMUSE journey books.
Give a wave to the aMUSE-ing Muses—and all
your personal muses who helped you every step of the way!
And have fun MUSE-ing about what you want your next role to be!